Stars

Heather Kissock
and Amy Duong

ALL ABOUT SPACE

LIGHTBOX
openlightbox.com

LIGHTBOX

Go to
www.openlightbox.com
and enter this book's
unique code.

ACCESS CODE

LBXL7996

Lightbox is an all-inclusive digital solution for the teaching and learning of curriculum topics in an original, groundbreaking way. Lightbox is based on National Curriculum Standards.

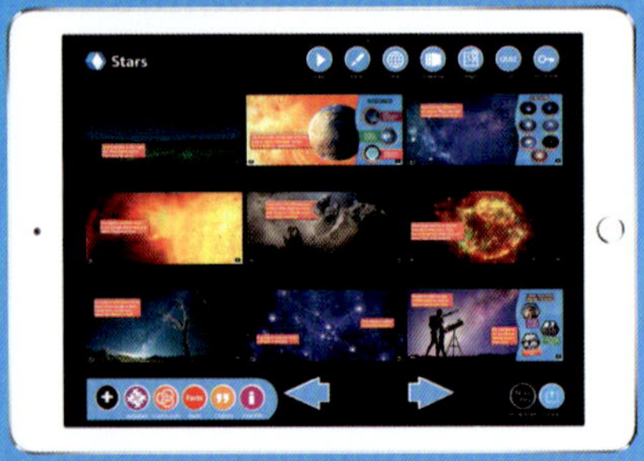

OPTIMIZED FOR

- ✓ TABLETS
- ✓ SMART BOARDS
- ✓ COMPUTERS
- ✓ AND MUCH MORE!

STANDARD FEATURES OF LIGHTBOX

- **AUDIO** High-quality narration using text-to-speech system
- **VIDEOS** Embedded high-definition video clips
- **ACTIVITIES** Printable PDFs that can be emailed and graded
- **WEBLINKS** Curated links to external, child-safe resources
- **SLIDESHOWS** Pictorial overviews of key concepts
- **INTERACTIVE MAPS** Interactive maps and aerial satellite imagery
- **QUIZZES** Ten multiple choice questions that are automatically graded and emailed for teacher assessment
- **KEY WORDS** Matching key concepts to their definitions

SUPPLEMENTARY RESOURCES

- **SHARE** Share titles within your Learning Management System (LMS) or Library Circulation System
- **CURRICULUM** Find national and state curriculum correlations
- **CITATION** Create bibliographical references following APA, CMSO, and MLA styles

VIDEOS

WEBLINKS

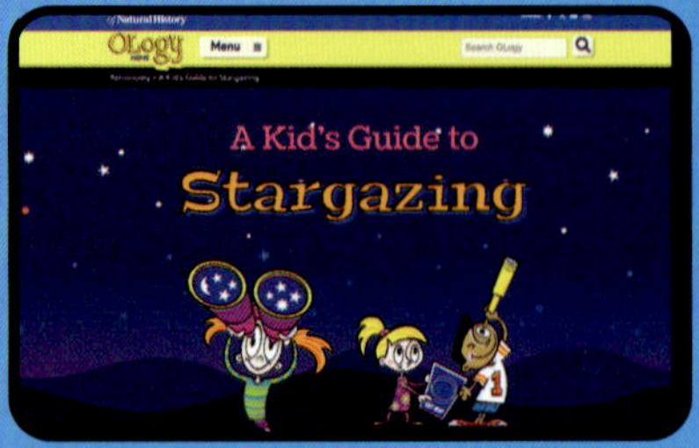

SLIDESHOWS

QUIZZES

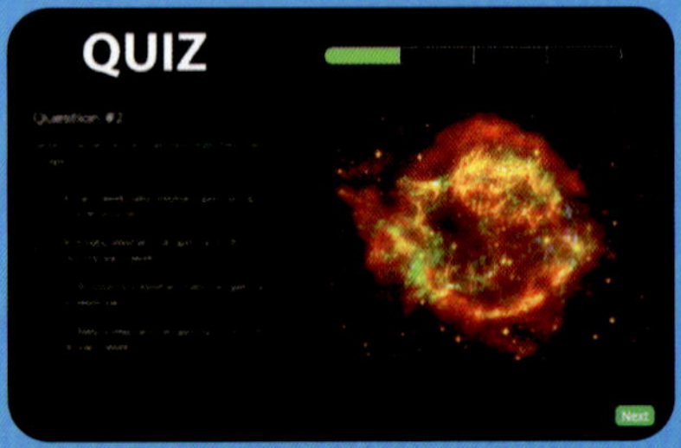

This title is part of our Lightbox digital subscription

Lightbox Grades K–2 Subscription
ISBN 978-1-5105-5423-8

Access hundreds of Lightbox titles with our digital subscription.
Sign up for a **FREE** subscription trial at **www.openlightbox.com/trial**

The digital components of this book are guaranteed to stay active for at least five years from the date of publication.

ALL ABOUT SPACE

Stars

CONTENTS

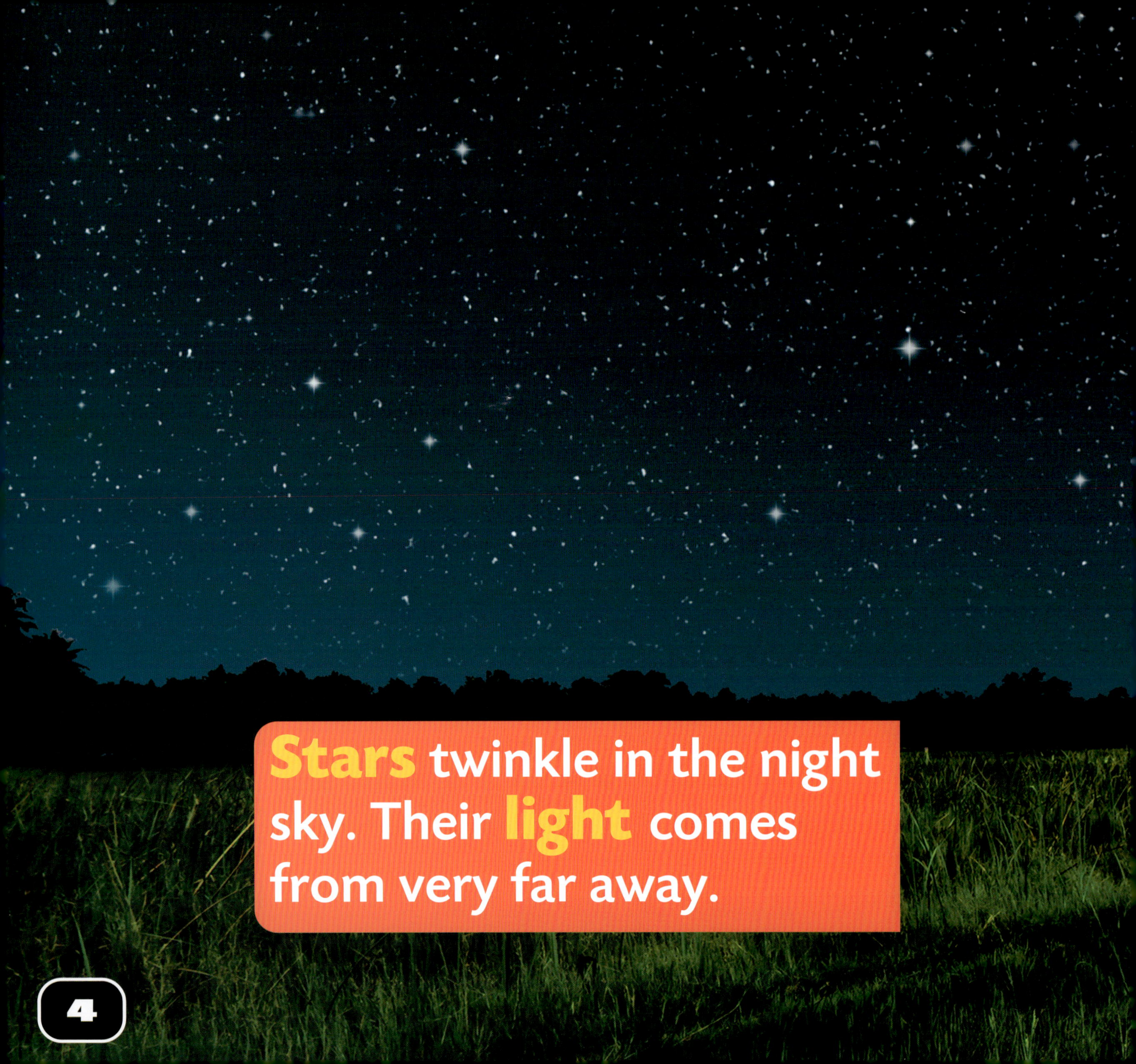

Stars twinkle in the night sky. Their **light** comes from very far away.

The **Sun** is the closest star to Earth. It takes **eight minutes** for the **Sun's light** to reach Earth.

COUNTING STARS

5,000
The number of stars that can be seen from Earth with the naked eye

4.24 Years
Time it takes light to reach Earth from its next closest star

12 Billion Years
Age of the oldest known star in the universe

Stars live for **billions of years**. They cool and change color over time.

STAR COLORS

Blue

Blue-White

White

Yellow-White

Yellow

Orange

Red

The Sun is a **yellow star**.
It will change into a **red star**
when it begins to cool.

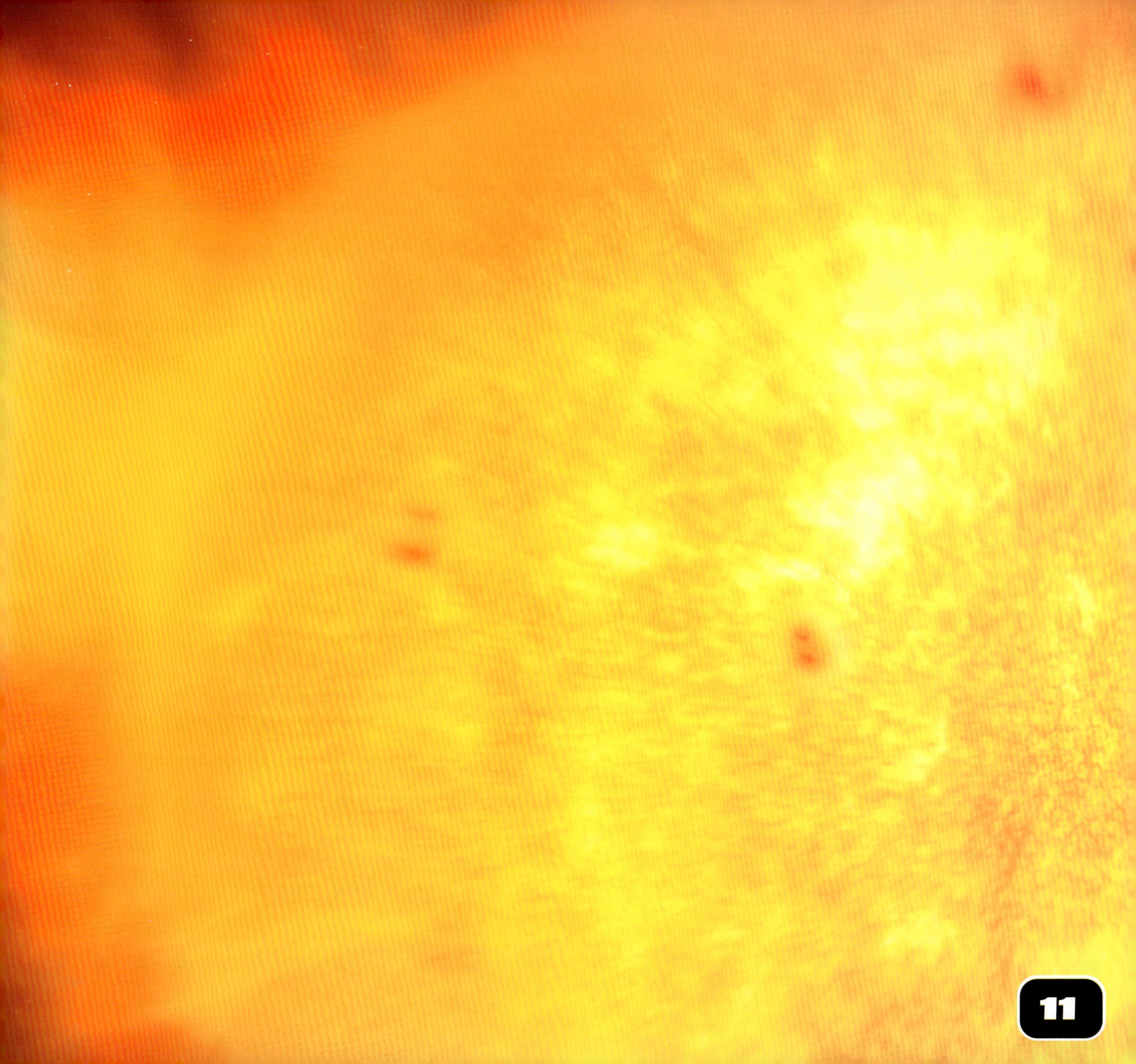

Some stars **shrink** and turn **white** when they are **very old**. They turn **black** when they **stop cooling**.

Most large stars have shorter lives than other stars. They **burn brightly** while they are alive. Then, they explode.

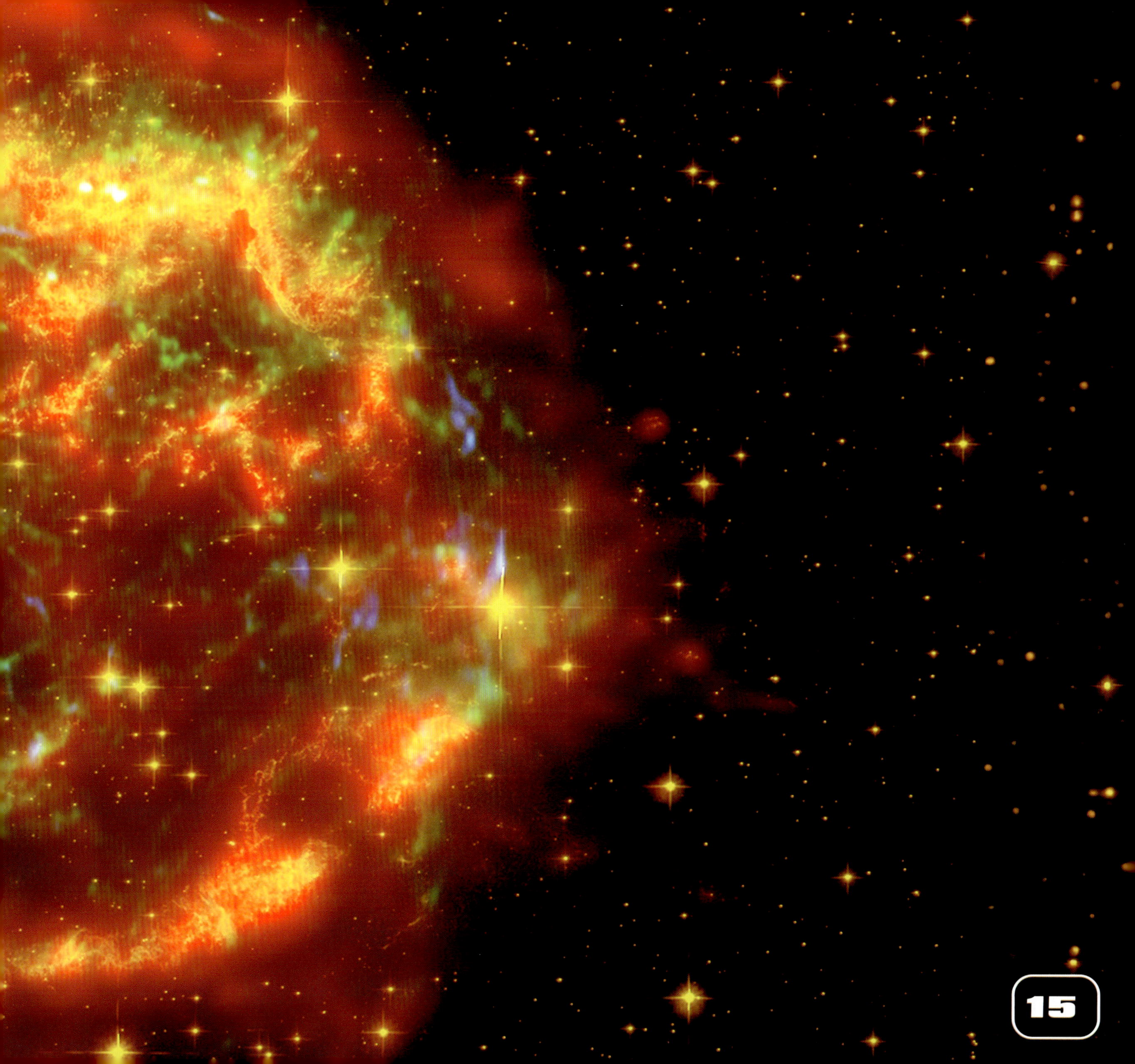

It is easy to **see stars** from Earth when the sky is dark. Fewer stars can be seen when the **Moon** is **full**.

A group of stars can form a **shape** in the sky.

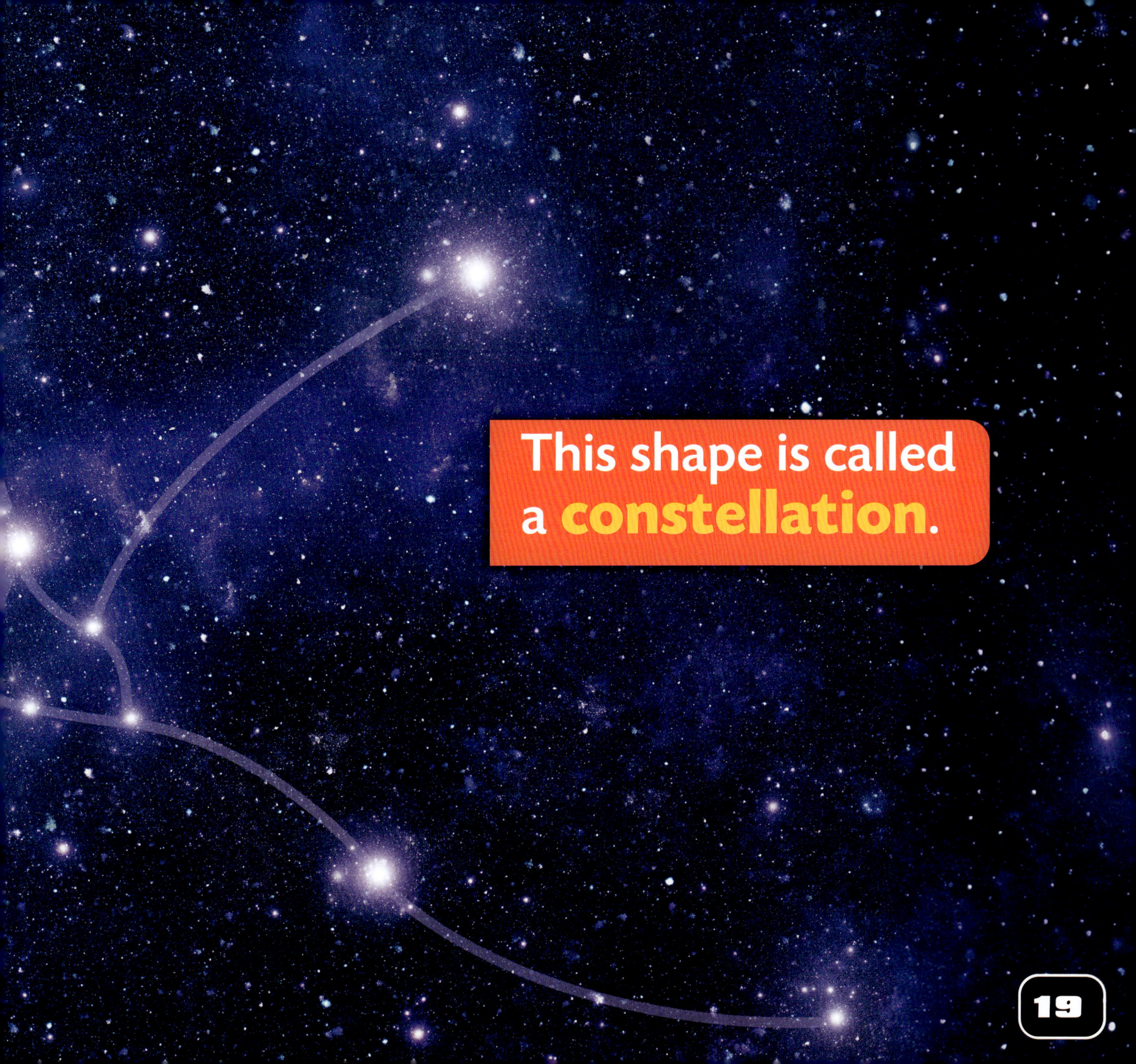

This shape is called a **constellation**.

People sometimes use a **telescope** to look at stars in the **night sky**.

LARGE TELESCOPES AROUND THE WORLD

No one knows for sure **how many stars** there are.

Mauna Kea Observatories, United States

Royal Observatory, Greenwich, United Kingdom

Paranal Observatory, Chile

STARS FACTS

These pages provide detailed information that expands on the interesting facts found in the book. They are intended to be used by adults as a learning support to help young readers round out their knowledge of space.

Pages 4–5

Stars twinkle in the night sky. Stars are made of gas and dust. They appear small from Earth because they are so far away. In reality, stars are very large. Many stars are much larger than Earth's Sun. The mass of some of these stars can be about 10 times greater than the Sun. Other stars are far smaller.

Pages 6–7

The Sun is the closest star to Earth. Earth is about 93 million miles (150 million kilometers) away from the Sun. Light from other stars takes longer to reach Earth because these stars are so much farther away. After the Sun, the closest star to Earth is Proxima Centauri. It is 24 trillion miles (39 trillion km) away.

Pages 8–9

Stars live for billions of years. Energy flows from the middle of a star. This keeps it bright. Stars are classified according to their color and luminosity, or brightness. Some stars appear less bright than they really are because they are farther away than other stars. The larger a star's mass, the shorter its life will be.

Pages 10–11

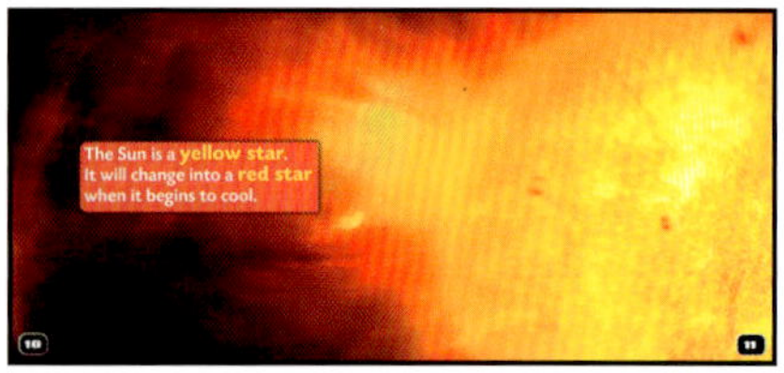

The Sun is a yellow star. Stars vary in color. The color they emit is based on their temperature. The Sun is a type of star called a yellow dwarf. As it cools, it will expand into a red giant before turning white. It will then become smaller.

Pages 12–13

Some stars shrink and turn white when they are very old. Stars change color and size as they age. When they first begin to cool, they may actually grow in size. As they burn off their gases, they begin to shed layers and change color. Most stars eventually turn black and die.

Pages 14–15

Most large stars have shorter lives than other stars. The most massive stars are called hypergiants. They are 100 or more times as massive as the Sun and emit much more energy. They burn this energy quickly, however, leading to a life span of only a few million years. Their lives end in a fiery blaze called a supernova.

Pages 16–17

It is easy to see stars from Earth when the sky is dark. Stargazers often travel to dark-sky preserves, far away from city lights, to view the night sky. City lights can block star visibility up to 200 miles (322 km) away. In the darkest locations, at least 2,000 stars can be seen with the naked eye.

Pages 18–19

A group of stars can form a shape in the sky. People in ancient times saw patterns when they looked up at the twinkling skies. They imagined lines that connected the stars. These lines formed shapes that are now called constellations. There are 88 different constellations in the sky. The northern half of Earth sees different constellations than the southern half.

Pages 20–21

People sometimes use a telescope to look at stars in the night sky. Like many stargazers, astronomers use telescopes to see distant stars. These large telescopes are housed in buildings called observatories. Arizona's Lowell Observatory, established in 1894, is one of the oldest observatories in the United States.

KEY WORDS

Research has shown that as much as 65 percent of all written material published in English is made up of 300 words. These 300 words cannot be taught using pictures or learned by sounding them out. They must be recognized by sight. This book contains 67 common sight words to help young readers improve their reading fluency and comprehension. This book also teaches young readers several important content words, such as proper nouns. These words are paired with pictures to aid in learning and improve understanding.

Page	Sight Words First Appearance
4	away, comes, far, from, in, light, night, the, their, very
6	Earth, for, is, it, takes, to
7	be, can, eye, its, next, number, of, that, time, with, years
8	and, change, live, over, they
9	white
10	a, begins, into, when, will
12	are, old, some, stop, turn
14	have, large, most, other, than, then, while
16	see
18	group
19	this
20	at, look, people, sometimes, use
21	around, how, knows, many, no, one, states, there, world

Page	Content Words First Appearance
4	sky, stars
6	minutes, Sun
7	universe
8	color
9	blue, orange, red, yellow
12	black
16	Moon
18	shape
19	constellation
20	telescope
21	Chile, Greenwich, Mauna Kea Observatories, Paranal Observatory, Royal Observatory, United Kingdom, United States

Published by Lightbox Learning Inc.
276 5th Avenue, Suite 704 #917
New York, NY 10001
Website: www.openlightbox.com

Library of Congress Control Number: 2024932121

ISBN 978-1-5105-8173-9 (hardcover)
ISBN 978-1-5105-8174-6 (static multi-user eBook)
ISBN 978-1-5105-8176-0 (interactive multi-user eBook)

Printed in Guangzhou, China
1 2 3 4 5 6 7 8 9 0 28 27 26 25 24

032024
110823

Project Coordinator: Sara Cucini
Designer: Terry Paulhus
Layout: Jean Faye Rodriguez

Every reasonable effort has been made to trace ownership and to obtain permission to reprint copyright material. The publisher would be pleased to have any errors or omissions brought to its attention so that they may be corrected in subsequent printings.

The publisher acknowledges Alamy, Getty Images, Dreamstime, and Shutterstock as the primary image suppliers for this title.